Living Life

POEMS TO LIVE BY

Paul Jones

Rushmore Press LLC
www.rushmorepress.com
1 888 733 9607

Copyright © 2019 by Paul Jones.

ISBN   Softcover   978-1-950818-22-8

All rights reserved. No part of this publication may be reproduced, distributed, or transmitted in any form or by any means, including photocopying, recording, or other electronic or mechanical methods, without the prior written permission of the publisher, except in the case of brief quotations embodied in critical reviews and certain other non-commercial uses permitted by copyright law.

Printed in the United States of America.

Some time when I lay down at night
I wonder if I truly have a reason to write
I still see the clouds I still hear the thunder
Where will the words come from I really wonder
Writing words is not like drawing a picture that can be traced
Writing words on paper need to come from your heart
need to come from grace
How do I begin how do I start
The words that I put on this paper must come from my heart
In order for me to put words on paper in order for me to write
I must see the words they must be in my mind's sight
When I was young I had no ideal of what I would do
I never thought of writing I never had a clue
Now that I sit here the words start to flow
But not to keep you on this one poem any longer
I must let you go

MATTERS OF THE SOUL

A Letter to A Son 3
Private Prison 4
A Lost Life 5
Hurting Man 6
Am I 7
Why Am I 8
Hurting Child 9
The Student 10
Emptiness 11
Emptiness II 12
The Sadness Within 13
Hurting Words 14
Little Boy 15
Overcoming 16

LIVING LIFE

A Letter to A Son

To be blessed with a son is a special deed
Now you must shape and mold your developed seed
It is more to being a father than just having a son
Having a son doesn't mean that your work is done
Let him run and play
But you must remember that young he will not always stay
After doing all that you can
You must not forget to show him how to be a man
You must teach and train
It is so much knowledge to be gained
His spirit and his life you try to build
So that one day he may be peaceful and tranquil
You must teach him that having a family must not be taken light
And that he should not run after the first fight
That providing for his family may not be a treat
But it might be up to him to make sure they have enough to eat
You must teach him that it is more to life than just growing old
That he must know that it is a place for his soul

PAUL JONES

Private Prison

We can all live in our own private prison
Your prison may or may not have bars
With or without bars they can both leave scares
We look over our lives and we seem to keep track
We know the things have we've done, the things that hold us back
We have things that we don't want anyone else to know
The things we try to hide the things we don't want to show
We all have done things in our past
But we are the ones that let those things last
You feel like you are the only one who has sinned
You feel like if anyone found out the world would end
Until that day you realize that you aren't the only one living behind bars
You are not the only one with hidden scares
Free is what you want to be
So you must stop looking behind and open your eyes to see
Take control of your life and bend the bars
You can then escape the internal scares

LIVING LIFE

A Lost Life

You put a gun in his hand
You tell him this will make him a man
You say, with us is where you want to be
But first you must take a life so we can see
A man falls to his knees
He starts begging please, please
But you pull the trigger with ease
So you just took a man's life without blinking
But deep inside you start thinking
They make you feel like you're strong
But deep inside you know that you were wrong
Now you're sitting in a jail cell in pain and aching
Because last night it was your manhood that was taken
You start to hang your head in shame
Thinking I took a man's life just to join a gang
You wait to hear from some of the other members
You wait through July, August all the way through December
You stayed here all of your life sentence
You have learned to ask the Lord for
forgiveness you have to learn about repentance
The family of the man's life you took
They have forgiven you because they live from the good book

PAUL JONES

Hurting Man

A man neglects his child
Now his child grows up wild
He has built up anger with his wife
Buried deep down inside has strife
So to hurt his wife he stabs their child with a knife
He was tired of hearing the child cry
So he stabbed him over and over
again, he wanted the child to die
The man is at peace
Because he thinks the crying has ceased
He lands himself in jail
With no one willing to make his bail
A day or two goes by
And then all of a sudden he hears a child cry
Crying the man cannot believe
In his mind he thinks am I being deceived
As he does everything to escape the sound
He starts to think to himself I am hell bound

LIVING LIFE

Am I

As I lay down looking toward the sky
Wishing only to die
Am I just being selfish
To be having such a death wish
Am I caring only about myself
Do I not care about anyone else
Am I not caring about my son
Or from the pressures of life am I trying to run
Am I caring about my friends
Or do I simply just want all of this to end
Am I caring about the love that I once had
Or for myself am I just feeling sad
Am I the one to end it all
Or should I just wait until I am called
Am I the one to say that it's a sin
To want all the hurt and pain to end
Am I

PAUL JONES

Why Am I

As the sun shines bright in the morning sky
I sit here with tears in my eye
Why do I sit here with tears running down
Disregarding all of the beautiful sights and sounds
The sun shines off my head with such a glare
As the wind blows gently through my hair
So why am I standing here with this tear
When I should be full of joy full of cheer
The grass in my yard is pretty and green
But yet a tear in my eye is still seen
In my fridge I have plenty to eat
All kind of food all kinds of meat
All of a sudden the tear starts to dry
I finally realize there is no reason to cry
I know that I am truly blessed
I was just feeling sorry for myself, I guess

LIVING LIFE

Hurting Child

My mind often wonders
Will I ever see through the clouds and thunder
A child shoots his mother
And then he shouts oh how I loved her
And when his mother dies
He sits there with tears in his eyes
But then not cutting any slack
Because all he wants another hit of crack
He's quick to blame the world for his problems
And now he thinks crack will solve them
He finally ends up in jail
But without a mother to make bail
He truly begins to feel the pressures of life
So he ends it all with a knife

PAUL JONES

The Student

As the clouds float through the sky not making a sound
I walk around campus with my pants hanging down
I look at myself and I think that I'm cool
While others look at me and say there goes a fool
I walk the halls not going to class
What is my class ranking, so what if I'm almost dead last
I've been accused of sexual assault and even rape
But each time I was saved by the cameras they allowed me to escape
They ask me when I get out what do I want to be
Well, who or what I want to be is a complete mystery even to me
My mom I thought was on my side
Because every time I did something she would just let me slide
The teachers, principals and even the police I've always out foxed
Until one day this bullet caught up with me and now I lay in a pine box
I know my mom will come in a shed a tear or two
This makes me wonder all the love she said that she had
For me was it really true

LIVING LIFE

Emptiness

If you look into my mind what would you see
A garden a yard or maybe a tree
When you look into my eyes is it a joyful tear
Or are they just full of fear
When you look at my lips do they speak words that you can trust
Or do they just speak out of lust
We all play little games
But are we really the same
We all have a role to play
And that role will decide if we are here to stay
When the end comes and the truth is told
Where will there be a place for your soul

PAUL JONES

Emptiness II

If you looked into my mind what would you see
A garden a yard or maybe a tree
Would it be full of flowers that bloom after the April showers
Or will it just stand alone
Without a friend without a home
When you look into my eyes is it a joyful tear
Or are they just full of fear
I look at you with tears in my eye
I say that I'm happy or do my eyes say that I lie
I say that our love will never stray
But am I just trying to get you to stay
When you look at my lips do they speak words that you can trust
Or do they just speak of lust
I tell you that my love for you is true
Am I just trying to get you to do what I want you to do
We all play little games but are we really the same
You tell me that there is no one
Are you telling me that so you can have some fun
We all have a role to play
That role will decide if we are here to stay
Only you can live your life
Only you can deal with the pains and strife
When the end comes and the truth is told
Where will there be a place for your Soul

The Sadness Within

The sadness the sorrow the hurt and the pain
Makes me think that I'm going insane
The little voices that are in my head
Makes me sometime wish that I was dead
As I take a good look back over my life
It is filled with so much hurt, sorrow and strife
I ask the Lord to lead me and guide me
I cannot help but to think that it's tomorrow that I might not see
I know that it's so much in life to be gained
But how can one tolerate so much hurt and pain
As I take a look into my mind
How come it's only the hurt and pain that I choose to find
How come the good is so hard to see
The good seems to run, to hide it seems to flee
As I live this life trying not to focus on the sorrow
I try so hard to live hoping for tomorrow

PAUL JONES

Hurting Words

Life is not full of flowers it is not a bowl of daisies
When I was yet a child I was called crazy
Sometimes I wonder by being called a name does it make it true
Does that name stick with you in your mind like glue
Maybe it wouldn't have hurt so bad if it was from some other
But when it comes from someone you trust and love like your mother
Now I must go through life with this insight
Not knowing if this is true or if she was right
Is this the reason that these thoughts keep feeling my head
Making me wish that I wasn't living wishing that I was dead
Sometimes I wonder, why did she do this to me
Was I not the child she wanted me to be
As I sit here with tears in my eye
I cannot help to think that maybe I should just die

LIVING LIFE

Little Boy

When I was a little boy some called me slow
As I got older my spirit started to grow
But I still had some to call me crazy
And then there were those that said that I was just lazy
But I had one that would not give up on me
He was the one at that time I could not see
All of a sudden it was like a light came on
All of the hurting words and negative talk was gone
And now I sit here with a college degree
This is something that they never thought would be
This is something that I never dreamed that I would see

PAUL JONES

Overcoming

As I walk through the valley of shadows of death
I can't help but to think of others as well as myself
I try to lay in peace but the crying seems to never cease
I look up to the heaven above
Hoping that I can enjoy and spread his love
Boys and girls live in sin
Only because they're trying to fit in
They say that joy comes tomorrow
But why must there be so much pain and sorrow

MATTERS OF THE HEART

Mother 19
Smile 20
Never Letting Go 21
Forever Love 22
A Confession 23
Magic Moment 24
Getting Married 25
Forget Me Not 26
Infatuated 27
Hard Pressed 28
Leave Me Alone 29
Precious Love 30
My Undying Love 31
Sealed with a Kiss 32
I Don't Know 33
First Love 34

LIVING LIFE

Mother

Once you lose a mother
You may discover that there is no other
You continue on with your life
You your sister brothers or wife
You may feel like you have nothing to lose
But to continue is what you must choose
You try so hard not to be mean
But you feel like you have no shoulder which to lean
You pray to God to help make you strong
While feeling like all the time you want to be alone
And when you are by yourself
You truly wish that you were with someone else
You suddenly realize that there is no other
That can take the place of your mother

PAUL JONES

Smile

If you put a smile on your face
You may or may not change the human race
If your face is wearing a frown
You may or may not bring the world down
When you're feeling lonely and blue
Just remember that to yourself, you must be true
You can do whatever you set your mind to
If only you will develop the attitude of can do
You think that you have to shove
But all you need to do is to trust and to love
You can be six feet four or five foot three
But if you believe in yourself you can be what you want to be

LIVING LIFE

Never Letting Go

There are not enough words to express how I truly feel
But you are worth more to than a million-dollar bill
The twinkle in your eye is like a burning fire
Deep inside it ignites my burning desire
Just by the touch your soft brown skin
Fills me with joy again and again
My heart skips a beat
When we are lying between the sheets
My love for you continue to grow deeper
This lets me know that you are a keeper

PAUL JONES

Forever Love

I surly hope you know what I mean
When I say that you beauty rises above cream
Your eyes are like two pearls
You are my world you are my girl
How much do I love thee
There are not enough ways to count
The only love that's greater is heaven fount
We may have had our ups and downs
But now our love is good and sound
When I close my eyes I can see your face
I know then that no one can take your place
So to end this poem the way that each day should start
I want you to know that you are always in my heart

LIVING LIFE

A Confession

I can't help but have this feeling in my heart
That you didn't want me from the start
And now that you must finally let go
It's your feeling that you want to show
Don't cry for me don't even shout
Because you are the one who choose to live without
Now that I'm gone
I don't want to hear any sad songs
If I wasn't so afraid
I would end it all with a blade
My life is filled with so much confusion
It makes me think that true happiness is all an illusion
As I sit in what appears to be a lonely cave
I'm thinking that it would be better just to be in my grave
Why living my life seem to be such a hard chore
But I know in my heart that I have a lot to live for

PAUL JONES

Magic Moment

From your beautiful smile
To your elegant style
From your jazzy talk
To your sexy walk
You are so lovely to me
You are someone I would love to wake and see
From the first time I saw you
I knew my feelings were true
You look like an angel from above
An angel that was sent to share my love
When we are together, we always share a laugh or two
Let us not forget the other thing we love to do
We laugh and play
Feeling like young we will always stay
I don't think there's anything wrong
By us having these feelings so strong
Sitting here looking at you with little to say
I hope that these feelings we have will always stay

LIVING LIFE

Getting Married

I love you is much too easy to say
Especially when your actions are pointing the other way
When we first met everything was great
But as time went on our love for each other seem to escape
Times may get hard and are so often unclear
We both know that it has a lot to do with nerves a lot to do with fear
We have to learn to trust and learn to share
Getting married was a way to show how much we care
As time goes by we might have a child or two
But we must not forget the things that we love to do
All we do is work so it might seem
But let us not forget the joy that being together can bring
As times get hard we often think about being free
But being together is better this we must agree
As time goes by and we both grow old
Our love will take the test of time and the truth will be told

PAUL JONES

Forget Me Not

When I am gone
I know that our love will continue on
The sun will not cease to shine
Nor will our love be left behind
I may not be there to dry the tears from your eye
I may not be there to hold you when you cry
Just remember those words that were nice and kind
The words that are stored deep so deep inside of you mind
I know that soon you will get a fresh start
And I know that I will always have a special place in your heart
Again my face you may never see
So all that I ask is for you to remember me
So when you look up at the blue sky above
Think about all the special moments we shared
And think about how you were truly loved

LIVING LIFE

Infatuated

I simply thought that it was infatuation
When I used to see you in my imagination
I used to think about you from head to toe
This is no line, this is the truth I hope you know
From your brown skin to your soft silk hair
I'm not a shame if you know how much I care
I look into your eyes so big and round
I can't hear anyone else I can't hear a sound
Your lips look as soft as the clouds above
They remind me of two precious doves
I look at you and try to stay sane
Because as of yet, I don't even know your name
How can I feel for you the way that I do
I do not know the answer I don't have a clue
I talk about you to all my friends
They tell me that I'm just dreaming again
I don't know what to do what to say
Maybe one day as I'm walking you will pass my way

PAUL JONES

Hard Pressed

For your love my body continues to yearn
When will I see when will I learn
That being with you is not a must
But it is my feeling that I must learn to trust
You left me a long time ago
For what reason I do not know
Yet my love for you is still
I do not know for what reason I guess it just my will
I try so hard to just let my feelings go
Just like the wind I wish they would just blow
Every time I hear or speak your name
My love for you returns as if it was the same
When I think about how beautiful our love could be
I just wish that it was something that both of us could see
I think it is better for us to stay apart
Who knows maybe someday we will get a fresh start

LIVING LIFE

Leave Me Alone

Why do I want to be with you
Do you know the reason do you have clue
When I'm with you I'm treated like a disease
Yet I continue to beg I continue to plead
You say that your love for me is true
But yet I really don't know what to do
My feelings for you I try so hard to hide
But you see right through you see deep down inside
Girl if you could only feel what I feel
Then you would know that my love for you is real
You think the words that I say are just lines
You may think all I want to do is bump and grind
Although my feelings for you are strong
I will not stay here and let you treat me so wrong
So when I close the door and tell you bye
You can simply walk out and continue to hold your head up high

PAUL JONES

Precious Love

As the sun comes up to shine
I thank the Lord every day that you are mine
They say that you can mail order a bride
I glad to say that I didn't have to because you came from deep down inside
The day that I met you I didn't have a clue
That the feelings and love we have would soon be true
When I first looked at your lips they looked ever so sweet
And now when I look at you the fire in me burns oh so deep
Just like a dog that loves his bone
I know that our love will carry on

LIVING LIFE

My Undying Love

My true love for you may be hard to express
But with these few words I will do my best
With each tear that falls, I promise that I will be there through it all
Just like the stars in the sky my love for you will never die
The beauty that you have I will always see,
It doesn't matter what difference may come or how old we may be
For all the things you've done for all of your headaches
I just want you to know how much of you I appreciate
Saying I love you is oh so true
But just saying those three words just simply will not do

PAUL JONES

Sealed with a Kiss

How can I express the way I really feel
Without making this a big deal
The thoughts of you warm up my darkest nights
You take away my biggest frights
You are as soft as the clouds above
It would be so easy for anyone to fall in love
But you know and I know that this may not be
But who knows we should just wait and see
Your eyes are like a burning fire
They can ignite my deepest desire
We were supposed to have passed like two ships in the night
But now I don't want to let you out of my sight
I hope that this poem doesn't push you away
Because friends and more I want to always stay
I pray that this poem lets you know how I feel
And now with a kiss I seal

LIVING LIFE

I Don't Know

When I look at you, you ignite my fire
You open up my deepest desire
I'm not sure if this is a feeling that I can trust
Or is it just deep-down lust
Your eyes are so dark they appear to glow
My body says yes but my spirit says no
I want so much for our bodies to touch
But wanting this might be a bit too much
I walk away with my head to the ground
Without telling you how I feel without making a sound
I walk away without looking back
Knowing if I do it will feel like having a heart attack

PAUL JONES

First Love

What in the world could be worse
Than to lose or leave the one that you loved first
You remember when your heart couldn't skip a beat
Because the words I love you, you just had to repeat
These words were ever so true
When you repeated over and over again, I love you
Planes my fall from the sky
But I thought you would always be the apple in my eye
Just assure as the sky is blue
I thought the love we had was really true
When I saw you with someone else it made me choke
I guess you know by now that my heart is broke
I try to keep my heart from turning into stone
Because I know after loosing you my life must go on

MATTERS OF THE SPIRIT

Resurrection 37
The Seed 38
My Dream 39
Leaders 40
Beach by the Sea 41
Seeking Help 43
His Words 44
His Grace 45
Walking by Faith 46
My Faith 47
Dying for Our Sins 48
Wondering Soul 49
What Is True Love 51
My Love 52
Music 53
The Message 54
God's Eye 55

LIVING LIFE

Resurrection

I looked inside deep into the ground
But yet my Lord's body was not found
There was a deep fear that came over me
I did not see whom I come to see
I could not move I could not stand
I was met by this being that I thought was a man
He asked me why do I cry why do I wipe
I replied I did not find the one I come to seek
He told me that there was no need to cry
He told me to dry every tear from my eye
He said the one that you seek is not here He is gone
He has ascended to his father He will not be there long
Then he said to me just as sure as my Lord was hung on a tree
To go tell His disciples and Peter to meet Him in Galilee
As two of the disciples walked along the way
They met who they thought was a stranger that walked with them that day
After they told the rest they did not believe
They thought in their hearts that they were being deceived
He sat down with them as they ate meat
Then they realized that this was Him whom they seek
He told them to go into the world and preach
To preach the gospel to everyone they reached
He then looked at his disciples all eleven
He smiled at them again and then ascended into heaven

PAUL JONES

The Seed

On the earth He placed His mighty hand
And from that touch was made the very first man
And with that man was laid a great foundation
One that was laid and developed into many nations
And in each man was planted a seed
But does a plant grow without any weeds
All he asked was that his commandment we keep
There would not have been any tears for us to weep
But even with only two
We found that so hard to do
We did not try to repent
But he blamed it on the help that was sent
From that point he let it in
He opened his arms and welcomed sin
From that sin was planted a curse
Passing through generation the curse grew worse
From lying to stealing to killing
When will it stop when will we start the healing
Plants find it very hard to grow
When will the healing start does anyone know
Many say that they believe
Do they really or are they once again tying to deceive

LIVING LIFE

My Dream

When the lights went out around midnight I still could see clear
I could not open my eyes I could not raise my hands
I thought of all of my works I thought of all my plans
It was truly midnight but yet I still could see
I saw two great gates I first thought they were for me
I tried to open the gates on my own
I knew I was built I knew I was strong
I saw someone with a book
But all I could do was to look
He asked my name and he asked what I have done
After being asked I realized that this was the one
I went down on my knees I began to plea
I heard a voice say look up and rise
Do you truly want to come inside
I said yes and that I had done my best
He stopped me and said before I let you start
I must look deep, deep inside of your heart
I began to think of all the things that I have done
In the name of lust in the name of fun
Them I knew he would surly push me away
And I would surly become a stray
The Lord I knew and the Lord I trust
But I also knew that I had done things out of lust
He said by your heart alone you are invited in
Because you all fall short and you all have sinned

PAUL JONES

Leaders

You have taught us what is pure and true
And it's not only what we say but what we do
You have taught us that what's in our heart we should believe
That it is in our emotions we can be easily deceived
You have taught that we can have all things of God that we seek
But first those things we must believe and speak
You taught us that if we live by faith and hold His words near
We do not have to live in doubt do not have to live in fear
You have taught us it is important to use our godly utilities
So that we can fulfill all of our godly abilities
You taught us that we should not compare ourselves to the rest
We should always concentrate on giving God our best
You have taught us that we might walk so long hard miles
But it's still ok for us to laugh and smile
You have taught us that in our heart we should not carry strife
For this we want to say thanks for giving us a brand-new life

LIVING LIFE

Beach by the Sea

As I walk on the beach by the sea the winds start
to blow a bitterly cold
I ask my Lord why you have forsaken me
As I walk on the beach by the sea
I suddenly hear a noise coming from the jungle
I tried to run but then I stumbled
As I walk on the beach by the sea
A deep fear swelled deep down inside
I wanted to run I wanted to hide
As I walk on the beach by the sea
I tried to yell I tried to scream
I wondered will I wake up is this all a dream
As I walk on the beach by the sea
All of a sudden I was pouring wet
I wondered was this the sea or was it just sweat
As I walk on the beach by the sea
I yelled my Lord why have you forsaken me
As I walk on the beach by the sea
I saw a friend fall to the ground
I called his name but there was no sound
As I walk on the beach by the sea
I looked around to see all that I could see
But all that I could see were bullets flying by me
As I walk on the beach by the sea

PAUL JONES

I felt a sizzling heat burning from deep inside
I wondered is this it have I too died
As I walk on the beach by the sea
I feel as if I'm all alone
Without any device or phone to call home
As I walk on the beach by the sea
Once again the winds started to blow
Where do they come from I do not know
As I walk on the beach by the sea
My feet were stuck in the pavement
As if I was planted in cement
As I walk on the beach by the sea
I told my home boy that I didn't want to go
But I couldn't turn him down I couldn't say no
As I walk on the beach by the sea
He told me that it would be a lot of fun
He said that we would be the only ones with guns
As I walk on the beach by the sea
Now all I heard was pop, pop, pop
And then all of a sudden, I saw him drop
As I walk on the beach by the sea
I hear a voice telling me that this does not have to be
If I would simply choose to not walk on the beach by the sea

LIVING LIFE

Seeking Help

When we first met you took on a heavy load
That's because you didn't leave your fear on the other side of the road
You keep refusing to give it all to me
But it's my love and grace that you long to see
By you trying to do things all in yourself
How can there be room for anyone else
It is time for me to do what I do
But if only you believe and trust that my word is true
I keep hearing you calling my name
But yet your situations are still the same
The freedom you seek are deep inside
But first you must be like a child just playing on a slide
You must learn to live and let go
This is when my blessing is free to flow

PAUL JONES

His Words

Listen to the words that come out of his mouth
You cannot tell if he's from the North or the South
His letters are not capital or bold
But they pierce deep, deep down into the soul
The words, how did He learn to speak
Those words they reach you even when you are sleep
Something feels wrong, something in your soul
You feel heavy as if you are about to explode
Your eyes begin to water
But you chant thank you father
He said that if you call my name
Nothing will ever be the same
The road that you traveled
It is long hard and full of gravel
He was pierced in his side
And all of your sins died
From our father He was sent
So that all we have to do is to believe and repent
For we are here on this earth for only a short time
Do you want to stay here, do you want to be left behind
The life you live is not your life to give
We look at the world but our eyes are closed
The unsaved one doesn't want us to see
He doesn't want to be exposed

LIVING LIFE

His Grace

The aches and pain they come to deceive
But by His stripe I was healed this I believe
As a bee gathers pollen to make his honey
We work and often dream of having lots of money
We are all told to sow seeds
But it is our almighty God who has taken care of all our needs
When we have learned to seek His face
We rest in knowing that we receive everything through His grace

PAUL JONES

Walking by Faith

The word tells us to walk by faith not by sight
It can be hard when all you see is boys and girls wanting to fight
The future can't be what this world is showing
Knowing who you are in Christ must be enough to keep you going
Then all of a sudden, a life is taken
But this one was a good one he had to have been mistaken
And to take his own life by his own hand
It's enough to make you wonder what's really going on man
But yet others walk around like there's nothing to do
They walk around without a plan without a clue
What is it going to take for some to open an eye
You know to open their eyes to stand up to even try
Try to understand that He is waiting for us to get in line
He doesn't want any of us to be left behind
It doesn't matter how young or old
He has already left to prepare a place for our souls

LIVING LIFE

My Faith

There's not anymore, a cloud over my head
Making me wish that I was dead
The sun has begun to shine
Leaving my past well behind
I can see through all the mumble
But yet I'm still able to remain humble
I know that my Lord has never lost a case
I know that I will always be saved by His grace
Although sometime is seems like I'm walking up a hill
I know that through my faith I can make it still

PAUL JONES

Dying for Our Sins

Lord I write this poem for you
Because it's only you that can do the things you do
You looked at someone like me
You showed me love you set me free
You instructed me with a mighty hand
But you say that your blessings are yes and amen
When my heart feels the hurt and pain
You remind me that I can always call on you again and again
Even when you knew that you were to be killed
You decided that it was not yours but it was His will
When satan had you hung upon that cross
It was then that he thought that our souls were lost
Into the pits of hell you descended
It was then and only then that all of our sins had ended
It was for all of our souls that you had to defend
Soon after that you decided to rise again

LIVING LIFE

Wondering Soul

This morning when I woke up I really wondered
I saw the clouds and I heard the thunder
I got up and I walked around my room
It was so cold and dark it was filled with gloom
I turned and looked at my bed what did I see
It was a silhouette and it looked just like me
I thought to myself am I being deceived
What is this what should I really believe
I continued on doing the things I had to do
I wondered what was for real what was really true
I shook my head to get the cob webs out
All of a sudden I heard a loud shout
I wondered who this could be
For there was no one else besides me
I wondered I had no clue
I wanted to leave I did not know what to do
The more I tried to run the more I tried to hide
Eventually I came to the conclusion that I had died
I looked around to see all that I could see
But all I could see was darkness looking back at me
All of a sudden a light started to shine
Was I going to heaven or was I going to be left behind

PAUL JONES

I tried to think back about all the things I use to do
But I still did not know I didn't have a clue
I heard a voice asking do you deserve this son
Why don't you tell me all of the things you've done
I did not know what to do I did not know what to say
I wanted to tell the truth and not let my answers stray
I remember some of the evil things that I have done
All in the name of lust all in the name of fun
I slowly held my head down to the ground
And thought that I was hell bound
When I looked up I saw the opened gates
I didn't know what to think it had to be a mistake
As I walked in I was greeted with a smile
I heard a voice say come on in you have walked some long
hard miles
When I walked in I saw all the beauty there could possibly be
I saw all the beauty that anyone could hope to see
But if asked what did it look like
It was if I lost my sight
To speak of a beautiful place is simply untold
You will just have to wait to discover the place for your soul

LIVING LIFE

What Is True Love

There was only one true love
And that love was from above
Jesus gave his life for us all
Because He knew that we would stumble and fall
From where does love come
It seems easier for others than some
We say that we love each other
But most can't even love their sisters or brothers
So, what is love how can we know
Why is it so easy to speak but so hard to show
I tell you that I love you
But how do we know that it is true
I say that my love for you is up to the sky
But for your love would I be willing to die
The gifts and money you will receive
Is this all a ploy to get you to believe
God gave up his only begotten son
Still we ask, what is love, are we all dumb

PAUL JONES

My Love

For my love you don't have to shove
All my love comes from above
For my gift you do not have to chase
For it is given to you with my grace
I did all I could while here on this earth
Did all I could from the time of my birth
I went to the wilderness to be tempted but he missed
But yet I was betrayed with such a simple kiss
I asked my father to remove this burden
But I knew it was my future I knew it for certain
They took me to their leaders they took me to their boss
They could not find any fault but I was still hung on a cross
They thought they killed me but I gave up my ghost
They started to gamble they started to boast
I went down in the earth I went down to the very end
I did this to save your lives to save you from sin
I ascended to heaven high up above
From up there I send you all of my love

LIVING LIFE

Music

We all listen to the music we choose
It doesn't matter if it's spiritual, gospel or blues
We all know Jesus can work it out
Which is enough to make us all want to scream and shout
Then we have I never would have made it
Which is enough to keep us going to not let us quit
Before the rap songs came that make us want to fight
It was the happy go lucky for our enjoyment Rappers Delight
And then we have songs to make you think that it's only for the lonely
But I'm here to tell you that the words are true that the kingdom
of God is for members only
There is no need to worry, ponder or stress
Because anyone can join all you have to do is to believe and confess
The Lord says to us to come one and all
You don't have to be lonely, chosen or called
When you feel like all you had and loved is gone and departed
You can turn to Him even if you are broken hearted
If you don't have a dime and you can't pay
You don't need any money you can come anyway

PAUL JONES

The Message

I give to you so you do not have to shove
I have given all of you all of my love
If you would simply stop focusing on your sins
And take a good look deeply within
When you look in the mirror you may only see your face
But if you look deep within you will see my grace
If I had not died upon that cross
Then you could say that your soul is lost
If you would only seek and believe
Then you would not so easily be deceived
Just like he declared his love with a dove
I'm still giving you my love from above

LIVING LIFE

God's Eye

When I looked up into the sky
I could have sworn that I saw God's eye
Although it was far away it wasn't hard to see
But the funny thing about it He was looking right at me
At first, I tried to run I tried to hide
Because I knew all that He could see,
He saw deep in me he saw inside
Then all of a sudden, I remember that Jesus was heaven sent
And all I ever had to do was to believe and repent
All of a sudden, I became brave
Because I remembered years ago I was saved

MATTERS OF LIFE

Broken Chains 59
Crossroads 61
Getting High 62
Keeping it Real 63
Solving Your Problems 65
Child Support 66
H.I.V 67
Death is in The Air 68
Friends? 69
Free 71
My Identity 72
Black Officer 73

LIVING LIFE

Broken Chains

As I lay down to sleep thinking about my week
I was suddenly wakened and treated as if I were a freak
I was bound in chains as if I had neither mind nor brain
They put me deep down in a boat
That was so hot and steaming the odor made me choke
I looked around to see all that I could see
But all I could see was darkness looking back at me
They took me off the boat as if I was an animal
If I would have stayed any longer I would have turned into a cannibal
They put me upon an action block
As if I were poultry or even live stock
They looked at my arms my legs my teeth
They looked at me as if I were a side of beef
I followed a man that was pale as snow
I did not know where he would lead me but I knew I had to go
I looked at the others the same color as I
But we did not dare to speak all we could do was sigh
I was forced up in the early dawn
Without my family without my son
I prepared my mind for a very long trip
But each time I ran they hit me on my back with a whip
Once again, I tried to run I tried to take flight

PAUL JONES

But I did not know to whom to turn for they all looked alike
At night when I had time look into the sky
I stared at the stars with tears in my eye
I stood as a strong figure of a man but broken hearted
Because all that I had known and loved was now departed
I wondered why did they do this to me
They took away everything that I loved to see
When I arrived here they called me wild
But they are the ones that stripped me away from my wife and child
I had to learn to deal with a lot of stress
Which in no way was this an easy task
Because each time I slipped
The taskmaster would laugh and crack his long, black, whip
They took my bright skinned brothers
And they told them that they were not like the others
They told them that they were better than the rest
Until they slept with their daughters and disturbed their happiness
They tried to take away my history
They wanted my past to become a complete mystery
In God's name in Jesus' name that I pray
That in bondage I will not always stay

LIVING LIFE

Crossroads

You travel the crossroads of time
Remembering what was left behind
Pondering what's ahead
Wondering just when you will be dead
So not to think of death
You try to enjoy the time that you have left
So, like a bird in flight
You continue to struggle and fight
Against the wind and rain
You decide to endure the joy and pains

PAUL JONES

Getting High

So you like to get high on drugs
You got so high that you burned the floor, you burned the rugs
You talk to a female trying to be sincere
She can't understand you because you are not very clear
Drugs make you high, they make you feel good
They make you feel like you can do things that you never could
You think that the dealers are good and kind
They sell you the drugs not caring about your mind
You buy the drugs until you run out of money
The dealer leaves laughing think that you are funny
To get more money you try to steal
You come to your senses thinking is this for real
So the habit you must try to kick
Thinking to yourself I have this licked
All of a sudden, your body starts to pain
So you take another hit thinking that you can sustain
You finally steal and you end up in jail
Now your body truly feels like you are in a living hell

LIVING LIFE

Keeping it Real

We all go through hurt and pain
But all in all we have so much more to gain
We love and we cry
I wonder if we will ever see through the clouds in the sky
You want a love like no other
You want a love that has not yet been discovered
You try to make up your mind to stay or go
You think, maybe you stay and just go with the flow
You stand in and you look outside
It would be so easy to just let things slide
You think that you have a love as deep as the earth's core
So why is showing it such a chore
The love that you are looking for has to be perfect
But if you found it could you handle it
There is only one such thing as a perfect love
The only true love comes from the heavens above
He loved us so much that he was willing to die
Now that is true love that is true love in anyone's eye
Try not to be so hard on yourself
Just take a look around look at everyone else
There is no need to be looking so low

PAUL JONES

With all of that beauty you should just let it show
A vision of beauty yes you are
Your beauty shines as bright as bright as the North Star
And your body is like a holy temple
They is no way that it could be just plain or simple
Just smile and let your ever-loving light shine
You will never have to worry about being left behind
What I have for you is a true passion
Do not mistake this for just an obsession
I am trying so hard to tell you how I feel
While at the same time I'm trying to keep it real

LIVING LIFE

Solving Your Problems

Trying to forget about the past
You drink a lot of beer
Knowing deep inside that this brings no cheer
You once had a love a love that you lost
You must now realize that this was no holocaust
A new love is found someone that truly loves you
But you push her away as if she has the flu
Deep inside you know that you were wrong
So now you drink a lot of beer trying to be strong
You say that you have changed that you are a new man
Have you really changed if so put do that can
Life can be beautiful and clear
If you would simply just put down that beer
When you find a new love try to stay involved
Then and maybe then your problem will be solved

PAUL JONES

Child Support

Why do you just want child support
So it's not the child but the man that you want to abort
You say just as long as he gives me my money
"I don't need a man honey"
Not really thinking about your child
Not even caring if he grows up wild
You say that you love your child with all of your heart
So how about helping him get a fair start
And you men should be doing everything you can
To make a difference to make a stand
You should not have to be made to pay
Because in your child's life you should always want to stay
How can you say that you don't care
When he has your eyes, your smile and yes even your hair
And when he grows up to be someone
You want to pump your chest and think "what a job I've done"
Both of you should work together to raise this child
And not let him grow up in the streets not let him grow up wild
So let's not worry so much about child support
And let's not worry about taking it to court
Because you're going to do all that we can
To help this young boy to grow up to be a man

LIVING LIFE

H.I.V

You take her home to your bed
While not really using your head
As time goes by you start to wonder did I make a mistake
Because all of a sudden you start to lose weight
You go to the doctor pouring with sweat
Waiting for the diagnosis with much regret
The doctor comes in and you fall to your knees
And then he tells you that you have H.I.V
And then your mind starts to wonder
Would this have happened if I had used a condom

PAUL JONES

Death is in The Air

Death is in the air
And some don't even care
Some people just point and stare
Death is in the air
Grownups laugh and play
While their children go astray
Death is in the air
Some think that on earth they will always stay
Thinking that times will always be gay
Death is in the air
Sex is no longer with the one you trust
It is now done out of lust
Death is in the air
As this poem comes to an end
Do you believe that you have been forgiven for your sins
Death is in the air

LIVING LIFE

Friends?

Through the storms through the rain
I feel so much hurt so much pain
When will this hurt and pain end
I tried so hard to turn to my friend
I thought he was the one that I needed to see
But it turned out that he would just turn his back on me
I thought for sure that he was my friend but then I was told
That he was no good and he was the reason that I was sold
He told the man that I did the crime
And now I'm locked up doing his time
I thought in my mind not my home boy
But he just tossed me away as if I was a used-up toy
For now, I sit behind these iron bars
While he's out riding around in his fancy cars
But there will be a day that I will get out
Then I will make him pay
I will make him scream, I will make him shout
Now I sit here with so much hate
At night when I lay here to sleep it is my man hood that they take
At first, I tried to scream I tried to fight
But sooner or later there was no more light
When I opened my eyes, I saw the doctor I saw the nurse
I started to scream I started to curse
How could this have happened to me
Why couldn't I have open my eyes why couldn't I see
I should have listened when I was told
To stay away from him he has a very bad soul
But I thought that I knew it all

PAUL JONES

But he was the reason that I would fall
All of a sudden, light comes on
I wasn't in prison I was at home
Was this a vision or something I would wake up to see
Or was it simply a warning that was meant for me
Today when my homeboy called
He asked me to go with him, with him to the mall
I thought about all the hurt and all the pain
I thought about the storms and all the rain
I told my homeboy that I wasn't going to go
My homeboy got mad but I still said no
He went anyway and he tried to rob a jewelry store
Be he got caught before he made it to the door
He tried to tell them that it was not his plan
He told them that I was the one I was the man
I was at home not even dressed
Then came a knock on the door I started to stress
They asked me if I knew my friend
I said yes, but our friendship had come to an end
I told them that he got mad today when he called
I turned him down I didn't go to the mall
They asked me if I knew what he was going to do
I told them that I didn't know I didn't have a clue
I asked them by the way where is he
They said that he tried to pin a robbery on me
You think that he's your friend, you swear to it, on your life
Until you turn around and he stabs you with a knife
And now you walk around mad
Because you don't have a friend that you thought you had
Your eyes are opened and you say never again
You will never call just anyone your friend

LIVING LIFE

Free

Freedom are we truly free
Or do we see what we want to see
We look and strain
Trying to point the finger of blame
We look at our kids with their pants hanging of their butts
They think that this is cool but it really sucks
They call themselves gangs
This is truly a shame
Free
How can we say that we are free
When we only be what others want us to be
We only imitate what we see
Even if it is off of black TV
Do we have our minds
Or are they only programmed with the times

PAUL JONES

My Identity

What do you do when you don't know who you are
When you look in the mirror you look from a far
You try to fulfill your life by buying a new car
But yet your life feels empty as empty as a jar
Not realizing how your past has left a deep scare
You turn to drinking you turn to the bar
By not knowing who to fight nor who to spare
You often wonder if you could have been in the movies
If you could have been a star

LIVING LIFE

Black Officer

A police officer shoots a child
And the public appears to go wild
A child turns around and shoots the police
Then all of a sudden, the noise seems to cease
Whites and blacks, they both call us n-----
Does that make it right for them to pull the trigger
With some blacks you try to help, you try to be on their side
But all they want is for you to let them slide
Your skin is black just like a lot of others
But that does not mean that you are all brothers
Some whites look at you as if you are an insect
They show you little mercy, they show you little respect
You're doing everything you can to stay honest and true
Because of your uniform, because of the blue
To the wrong you try not to yield
Because on your chest you wear the shield

JUST MATTERS

The Cloud 77
Feeling Different 78
Joy and Pain 79
Star Maker 80
Nellie 81
My Queen 82
Child Hood 83
The Future 84
Unwanted Guest 85
Why We Celebrate 86
My Present 87
The Words That I Write 88
Once a Year 89
The City 90

LIVING LIFE

The Cloud

The cloud that hangs over your head making you wish
that you were dead
Is the same cloud that hung over you as a girl or boy
But then it brought you shade it gave you joy
The difference is that now the pressures of life
may seem to make you choke
But Jesus said all that is heavy burden that up my yoke
We try to carry all of our problems and our worries on our
shoulders
Until they start to feel like Mount Rushmore heavy as
boulders
We want all of the pressures of life to just cease yet we seem to
forget
That Jesus came, died and rose so that in him we may have
peace
We put pressure on ourselves by looking ahead
And not taking the time to enjoy the moments we have
instead
For God so loved the world that he gave his only begotten son
If we could only rest in that we would realize that
all of our works has been done

PAUL JONES

Feeling Different

As I sit here and wonder, am I going insane
Is this life reality or is it all just a game
If a game then who is it to blame
Or do I just hold my head down in shame
I feel like a blah of ink just a simple stain
My life I try to live, teach and train
I often live my life I often feel the drain
But yet deep inside I know that I have so much to gain
A decision I have to make to live my life or to live in pain
Or should I just sit here and wonder, wonder if we are all the same

LIVING LIFE

Joy and Pain

I started off writing about hurt and pain
Not really knowing how much I had to gain
As I look up in the sky above
Now I realize what's love
A lot of mistakes I have made in my life
I have lusted, cursed, I have even had strife
The hurt and pain seemed oh so real
I can now truly say that it was no big deal
I have lost things that I considered close and dear
Things that made me sad things that made me drink lots of beer
But for me to continue on he gave me a shove
He gave me a shove by letting me know that I am loved

PAUL JONES

Star Maker

At night when I look into the sky
I look up there with tears in my eye
It reminds me of a cold dark gloomy room
Full of sadness full of gloom
I wonder what I can do to make it bright
Something to bring some joy something to give it some light
I told my friends that I could do just that
But they didn't believe they said that I was a faker
But if they only knew that I was the star maker

LIVING LIFE

Nellie

As the lighting clashed and the thunder pounded
I thought in the woods I heard a sound
I went in there to see what I could see
What I saw was two big beautiful eyes looking back at me
As I stood there my coat started to leak
She stood there as if she wanted to speak
I took her to my home I wanted her to stay
But just as soon as the weather broke she ran away
I did not want her to leave I didn't want her to go
I don't know why but I searched high and low
My search took me into the nearest town
I listened for her crying I listened for a sound
Just as soon as I was about to walk away
I heard a familiar sound I heard her sweet nay
I grabbed her and gave her a hug and rubbed her belly
I will name her after my dear departed
And I will call her Nellie

PAUL JONES

My Queen

I sit in my beautiful house all alone
While all of the time wishing that I could go home
I truly miss all of the things we use to do
You know the garden the yard and even the Pine tree
Yes I can still see the garden yard and even the tree
But it's not the same not the same to me
I remember how we used to have fun
Just running playing and relaxing in the sun
I look into all of my rooms
They are filled with emptiness loneliness and gloom
They say that home is in the heart
I guess that I really need a fresh start
When I close my eyes I can still see her face
I don't know if another could ever take her place
I tried to replace her with several others
But replacing her is no easy task this I have discovered
From my topic I try not to stray
But I can't help but to think how we used to play
Her hair was black, black as the darkest pearl
She was my friend she was my girl
This relationship may not be as it might seem
But I can assure you that she was my little black Queen

LIVING LIFE

Child Hood

I remember back in the days
You didn't have to worry about sex
You didn't have to worry about Aids
I remember when you use to have fun
Just by going outside playing and relaxing in the sun
I remember when brothers and sisters use to be friends
You know the type that you can count on again and again
I remember when songs use to have meaning
Not just a lot of crap and screaming
So when you're dead and you're gone
Will you leave fond memories to carry on

PAUL JONES

The Future

I see the world and it looks like it is ending
I wonder will there be a new beginning
I see us fighting many wars
So what is there anyone keeping up with the scores
A plant withers up and die
Because the soil is too hard and dry
Boys and girls both live in sin
Only because they are trying to fit in
The days are dark much like the night
You can forget all about any sunlight
I sit in dark and gloomy room
Wondering if we are truly doomed

LIVING LIFE

Unwanted Guest

You turn on the lights and we begin to scramble
Maybe we like to play Russian Rolette maybe we like to gamble
We eat what you eat and even what you don't
You want us to just leave but you know that we won't
We wait until someone comes over, you know like a friend
And then we appear again and again
You spend all of your money on different cans of spray
The smell of the spray makes us want to stay
You sit down with your friend to play some spades
He kindly suggest that you need some cans of Raid
We look at him as if he has walked into a trap
For that suggestion we jumped up and gave him a pimp slap
He looked over at the sink and saw us floating on our boat
He screamed this is enough and grabbed his coat
We wonder what took him so long
Oh by the way we are glad he's gone

PAUL JONES

Why We Celebrate

From the heavens opening up to sing
To being given presents from many kings
When I looked down upon His glorious face
I felt His love, I felt His grace
Although He was only a very young child
Deep down inside He made my heart smile
They say that our savior was born in a manger
Maybe it is for this reason that He has never met a stranger
So, as we go out to buy gifts, gadgets and toys
For our little girls and our little boys
Let us not forget the Jesus is the turn reason
Why we celebrate this joyous season

LIVING LIFE

My Present

I hung my stockings by the tree
While hoping that Santa remembers me
Come on Santa don't be late
I left you milk and cookies on the plate
I hope you got the letter I sent
Because all I asked for was one present
I closed my eyes and pretended to go to sleep
It seemed to take days it seemed to take weeks
I hope that the present that I asked for is the present that I get
Because all that I asked for was a shining new corvette

PAUL JONES

The Words That I Write

The words that I often write
Who are they to say if they're wrong or right
I see the clouds and I hear the thunder
Where do the words come from I often wonder
Where will I get the words where do I start
The words that I write must come from my heart
When I write the words and I try to be great
The words don't come out right they come out as fake
When I relax and put self aside
It's like when my pen hits the paper it just glides

LIVING LIFE

Once a Year

They say that Christmas only comes once a year
I say that every day we should be full of joy and cheer
Each day we are given we should love and hold dear
Even if a love one is gone, it's in your heart that you keep them near
Sometime life may seem so hard this is how things can appear
But when they do remember you can take a look back into the rear
I want to tell you what Christmas means to me
It's a day that when I was a young child, I would love to see
Sometime we would have presents under the tree
And sometime we would just be happy of what day it would be
No presents under the tree did not stop the happiness
the fun didn't cease
Because mom always made sure that we had a wonderful feast
Now that time has passed, I barely can remember one Christmas
from the last
Time seems to go by so fast
It seems like over my eyes a shadow has been casted
So now I realize where I am in this place
I know now that I celebrate Christmas because of His grace
I celebrate more than a baby lying in a manger
I celebrate because He came to save us from all
Hurt, harm or danger
So, when someone looks at you and say Happy Holidays
You can proudly say it's because of His birth
that I remember Him always

PAUL JONES

The City

Crime is around every corner on every street
IN THE CITY
There are neither children playing nor sunlight shining
IN THE CITY
The creatures and critters that once ruled the night
Now appear in very dim light
IN THE CITY
A day may come a day may pass
But you are unable to tell this one from the last
IN THE CITY
A place that was once prolific in progress
Is now in turmoil and depressed
IN THE CITY
With clouds always in the sky
Most humans wishing only to die
IN THE CITY
There is plenty water around but none to drink
Because it is filled with corpse and stink
IN THE CITY
Living is not easy in fact it's very hard
For those that remain it's even a job
IN THE CITY

LIVING LIFE

You must do all you can to stay alive
You might even have to kill to survive
IN THE CITY
The odor is an awkward smell
It is enough to make you think you were in hell
IN THE CITY
The garbage you have to dig deep
Just to find you enough to eat
IN THE CITY
Only the strong know how to survive they have the might
They have the will they know how to fight
IN THE CITY

Paul Jones was born in Pine Bluff Arkansas. Although born and raised in the South, his experiences have taken him as far away as California, Germany and Honduras to name a few. He has over fourteen years in the United States Armed Forces, as well as over twenty-three years in law enforcement. As a law enforcement officer, he has served as a member of S.W.A.T, bike patrol, school resource and a director of security for a local high school. He has also received many awards.

While residing in Pine Bluff, he is an active member of his church community. He is a sport car enthusiast, as well as a husband, father and a mentor to youth. He is also available for interviews, book signings, and public speaking.

www.ingramcontent.com/pod-product-compliance
Lightning Source LLC
Chambersburg PA
CBHW020126130526
44591CB00032B/549